The Little Book of

Arsenal

Edited by

NICK CALLOW & NEIL MARTIN

CARLTON
BOOKS

First published by Carlton Books 2002

A CIP catalogue record for this book is available from the British Library.

ISBN 1 84222 672 X

Printed in Singapore
3 5 7 9 10 2 4 6 8

INTRODUCTION

People say that footballers speak with their feet and that is certainly true of those who have played for Arsenal, but as these quotations show, they and many others connected with the club can utter one or two words worth listening to when necessary. For new fans and life-timers, here are some of the gems from the great and the good who have passed, and continue to pass, through the fabled Marble Halls of Highbury.

Whether you want to discover the real reason behind Charlie George lying down in the centre circle after scoring his Double-winning goal in 1971, or who prided himself on scoring good own goals, this is the place to find out.

From literary giants to illustrious fans, from one club record-breaker to another – for them, and everyone devoted to the club, there is only one Arsenal.

❝ I am going to make this the greatest club in the world. **❞**

Herbert Chapman
sets the standards in 1925

'There are two kinds of visionary:
those that dream of a whole new
world, and those who dream of
just one thing. Chapman's vision
was of the greatest football team
in the world. His genius was
actually creating something
close to that.'

Bernard Joy

'My aim is simple – to make Arsenal not just the best in the Premiership, but the biggest and best club in the world.'

Arsène Wenger *continues the theme some 70 years on*

Arsenal

❝The club is so superbly run. They say a swan serenely glides across the water and underneath it is paddling like mad. At Arsenal they don't even have to paddle, they just glide.❞

Malcolm 'Supermac' MacDonald

❝When you grow up with a
club and you end up playing
for them and winning things,
you are from that club. I was
produced here. I was
formulated here.❞

Liam Brady

‟With a great name like ours only success is good enough.„

Don Howe, *now Youth Coach, continues to demand the best*

'Keep up your reputation for sportsmanship. Don't barrack the referee.'

Tom Whittaker *addresses the Highbury crowd in 1947*

❛Herbert Chapman worked himself to death for the club and if it is to be my fate I am happy to accept it.❜

Tom Whittaker *as he takes over as manager*

❝It works. I am just waiting until everybody has copied it, then I shall come up with something new.❞

Herbert Chapman *explains his famous 'M' formation*

Arsenal

'We are going for the
Double. There is real
character in this side and
now we are going to
show we can win League
and Cup.**'**

Frank McLintock *after the semi-final replay v Stoke*

❝I would not normally say this as a family man, but I am going to ask you for the sake of this football club, to put your family second for the next month. You have the chance to put your names in the record books for all time.**❞**

Bertie Mee *to his players in run-in to the Double*

"Arsenal have got as much chance of being handed the title by Spurs as I have of being given the Crown Jewels. They are the last people we want winning the Championship. Now we mean to round off our season by beating Arsenal."

*Tottenham captain **Alan Mullery** sets himself up for a fall in 1971*

❝ There was no way we were
going to be beaten. **❞**

Bertie Mee *on the same game*

"I put everything into every game I played for Arsenal. As captain, I was motivating the side throughout every 90 minutes in front of 50,000-plus crowds every time we played."

Frank McLintock

❝My thoughts turned straight to the Cup Final and I was worried the crowd might injure our players. Some wanted their boots, which of course they had to wear on Saturday.❞

Don Howe *plays down the celebrations – there was still the Cup to be won*

'People say why did I lie on the floor after the goal, they said I was tired. But I think I was a lot cleverer than people thought.'

Charlie George *reveals it was all a time-wasting plan after scoring the Double winning goal*

❝My first football memory was Charlie George's goal to win the Double in 1971. After that game I decided to become an Arsenal fan.❞

Paul Davis

I was like an empty shell after giving everything on Monday night and was so whacked that it was almost as if it was someone else lifting the FA Cup.

Frank McLintock

"They talk about Bobby Moore and Dave Mackay as great captains, but for my money McLintock is more inspiring than either of them. I am beginning to feel obsolete in the dressing room."

Don Howe

Above all we were blessed with a backbone of men with character who demanded excellence from others.

Don Howe *in 1971*

‘ Winning the title against Spurs
was obviously nice, but I just
remember the Championship
race being constant hard graft.
And the FA Cup Final... was just
a non-event as far as I was
concerned... I can't say I
particularly enjoyed that day. ’

Peter Simpson *shows you can't
please everyone*

❛The bloke who owned the Wimpy bar at Finsbury Park, where we all used to go on a Friday morning, said, "I'll give fifty quid to anyone who gets a hat-trick." And bosh, straight away – he was a bit sick. I didn't keep it all, Ian Ure made me split it.❜

John Radford *recalls a hat-trick in four minutes against Bolton in the FA Cup*

❝The first man in a tackle never
gets hurt.**❞**

Wilf Copping

'When I am asked why I stayed so long the answer is simple, I never wanted to be anywhere else. I could have earned a lot more by moving, but that wouldn't compensate for all the good years with a great club.'

David O'Leary *on what drove him to break George Armstrong's Arsenal appearance record*

' If I've got a good goalkeeper and a good stopper centre-half, all I need is the two best wingers and the best centre-forward there is. It doesn't matter what the rest are like. **'**

Herbert Chapman

❝When I first came to Arsenal I realised the back four were all university graduates in the art of defending. And as for Tony Adams, I consider him to be a professor of defence.❞

Arsène Wenger

'I made Tony Adams one of the youngest captains in Arsenal's history and I never had any doubts about him doing the job. The modern game is short of dominant personalities, so Tony stands out like a beacon.**'**

George Graham

As far as I'm concerned, Tony [Adams] is like the Empire State Building.

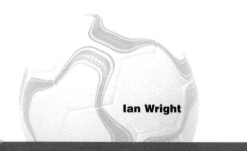

Ian Wright

❝I play on the right, Tony
on the left and we'll deal
with whoever comes
along, big or small.**❞**

Martin Keown

❝ He is a truly magnificent 'keeper. I am lucky to play in front of him every week. You look over your shoulder and feel safe. When I started playing for Arsenal I thought that if the ball went past me it would be a goal. I still go out with that attitude but with David behind me I know I don't have to sell myself. **❞**

Tony Adams *on David Seaman*

'It doesn't really matter if it's
a back four or a back five.
The most important thing is that
all of us have the same attitude
to defending, which is an
absolute determination to keep
a clean sheet.'

Martin Keown

❝I think I lost my barnet [hair] flicking the ball on for all them years at the near post from Brian Marwood's corners.**❞**

Steve Bould *on Arsenal's prolific corner routine*

"I've never been a goalscorer, only own goals. Good own goals."

Steve Bould

❝The star of the season was
the squad.**❞**

Arsène Wenger *at the*
end of 2001–02

There wasn't a lot of support, so I thought, "Why not," and next thing I knew it was in the back of the net.

Ray Parlour *explains his opening goal in the FA Cup Final 2002*

" The perfect end to a perfect campaign. "

*Comment in the **Daily Mail** after Arsenal complete the Double on 8 May 2002*

❝We love you Freddie because you've got red hair. We love you Freddie because you're everywhere. We love you Freddie 'cos you're Arsenal through and through.❞

Arsenal supporters *show their appreciation of Freddie Ljungberg's contribution to the 2001–2002 season*

Arsenal

"If you selected a team of nice people, Dave Rocastle would be captain."

David O'Leary *on the death of David Rocastle, March 2001*

❝ George Graham was telling Lee Chapman that if footballers looked after themselves there was no reason they could not play until 35. Then he looked over to me and said, "Well, maybe not you, Quinny." ❞

Niall Quinn *recalls a much earlier conversation with his old Arsenal boss having broken the Republic of Ireland scoring record at the age of… 35!*

I didn't score as many
as I hoped, but it was
nice that I always seemed
to score against
Tottenham. **"**

Charlie Nicholas

❝ In my time players had short hair, wore long shorts and played in hobnail boots. Now they have long hair, short shorts and play in slippers. **❞**

'Gentleman' Jack Crayston

❝The greatest one player over the years has to be Liam Brady. He is simply the best player I have ever seen in an Arsenal shirt.❞

Tom Watt, *actor and radio presenter*

It was a tragedy of
monumental proportions
for the club.

*Manager **Terry Neill** after Liam Brady joins Juventus*

'There's a minute left on the clock, Brady for Arsenal...right across, Sunderland...It's there, I do not believe it, I swear I do not believe it!'

Peter Jones *commentates as Arsenal score the winner in the 1979 FA Cup Final against Man United*

❝I think without doubt that
Dennis Bergkamp is the greatest
player to have played for Arsenal
in the last 30 years, for as long
as I can remember.❞

Liam Brady

'Other clubs never came into my thoughts once I knew Arsenal wanted to sign me.'

Dennis Bergkamp

❝If Ryan Giggs is
worth £20 million,
Bergkamp is worth £100
million.**❞**

Marco Van Basten

❝I started clapping
myself, until I realised that
I was Sunderland's
manager. **❞**

Peter Reid *after Dennis Bergkamp scores*
against Sunderland

❝I've trained against the likes of Dennis Bergkamp and that can make you quite nervous.❞

*Young 'keeper **Graham Stack** reveals how even in training Dennis Bergkamp is to be feared*

❝I saw John Jensen
score for Arsenal.**❞**

Fans' T-shirt *after John Jensen finally scores in his*
98th game for the club

**'You can attack
for too long.'**

Herbert Chapman

❛Coupled with his sincerity and his loyalty to all his bosses, he had a trait few of us are blessed with – an ice-cold temperament.❜

Tom Whittaker *on Cliff Bastin, previous holder of Arsenal's goal-scoring record*

❛The Third Division
footballer may not be a
soccer artist, but when
it comes to the heavy
tackle, he ranks with
the best.**❜**

Cliff Bastin *following Walsall's shock 2–0 win
over Arsenal in 1933*

❛The centre-forward's drunk, Mr Allison.❜

Ted Drake to manager George Allison after he had just downed a bottle of lemonade that was being used to highlight tactics

❝ For you lad – and
there's no hard
feelings. **❞**

Aston Villa players *having signed the
match ball for Ted Drake after he had scored
seven goals against them in 1935*

" To be mentioned in the
same breath as Ted
Drake and Cliff Bastin is
a great honour. **"**

Ian Wright *becomes Arsenal's record goalscorer*

'What's it like being in Bethlehem, the place where Christmas began? I suppose it's like seeing Ian Wright at Arsenal.'

Bruce Rioch

"My image of the day will always be of the joy of the whole team when he broke the record. That shows how he is accepted by everyone. It was an historical moment. Maybe it will be 100 years before the record goes again. After all, it has stood for so long and Arsenal had some great strikers."

Arsène Wenger *on Wright's goalscoring record*

'The English players can do a lot for the French guys when they come. We can let them know what they're in for.'

Lee Dixon

❛We won the league at Old Trafford, we won the league in Manchester.**❜**

Arsenal supporters *reflect on the achievements of 2002*

"We won the league
on the Mersey, We won the
league on Merseyside."

Arsenal supporters *reflect on the
achievement of 1989*

' Good old Arsenal, we're
proud to say that name,
While we sing this song we'll
win the game. **,**

Arsenal supporters

❝Christ, they've only lost one game. When was the last time that was done, a hundred years ago?**❞**

Sir Alex Ferguson *can hardly believe Arsenal won the League in 1991 losing only once*

❛Arsène who?**❜**

Tom Williams, *a lifelong supporter, reacts to Arsène Wenger's arrival on the back page of the* Daily Express

❛When he arrived, it was
Arsène who? But I had seen
this guy at close quarters.
I had seen him work at
Monaco, seen how he dealt
with players and the public
in general.❜

David Dein *sets the fans straight*

❝He has given us
unbelievable belief.**❞**

Paul Merson *on the impact of Arsène Wenger*

❝I think in England you eat too much sugar and meat and not enough vegetables. It's silly to work hard the whole week and then spoil it by not preparing properly before the game.❞

Arsène Wenger *gets out the broccoli and prepares to change the diets of Arsenal players forever, October 1996*

It is new to me to have someone checking your diet and giving you all kinds of tips – what to eat, when to eat, how to chew, when to eat chicken, when to eat fish, when to eat meat. You would think that is easy.

Giovanni van Bronckhorst

❝He is a hybrid. He is highly intelligent – he speaks five or six languages. He is cool, calm and collected, a great tactician. He also knows a lot about medicine. It's very rare that you find all that in a manager.❞

David Dein *continues to make his point about Arsène Wenger*

❝Sometimes there is nothing better in life than being a Gooner.❞

Kevin Campbell

‘ Going to matches at Highbury is like visiting church, it's the stuff of sustenance for the community's infrastructure. I love it on matchdays when the whole area becomes a sea of red. It's a special thing. **’**

David Soul, *aka Hutch, gets the Highbury bug*

‘Tottenham tried to sign me but I held off and came to Arsenal because Arsène Wenger was here.’

Emmanuel Petit

&Petit borrowed cash from Alan Sugar to take a cab to Highbury and sign for Arsenal.&

It gets even better – *a newspaper headline on Petit's route to Highbury*

❝He took time to understand me, to understand my wild side. He worked on my psychology. He spent many hours talking to me and he understood what I could and could not do. When I think about what I could have become, I owe everything I am now down to Arsène. He is the greatest man I know.❞

Emmanuel Petit *gets some help from Arsène Wenger*

" If a player doesn't like playing over winter and thinks there should be a winter break they shouldn't go to England. That's the way they play the game there and it's no secret that you have to play some tough games in tough conditions. **"**

Marc Overmars *on foreign players moaning about playing in England*

❝All Europe thought Overmars was dead because of his damaged knee. But in every important game we have had this season, he has scored. He has got great mental strength. He is a world-class player.❞

Arsène Wenger *after the 1998 FA Cup Final*

❛Seriously, I was the only player at Ajax who used to have fried eggs for breakfast everyday. It's one of my superstitions. If I don't have a fried breakfast in the morning, I won't play or train well.❜

Marc Overmars' *secret to scoring the Double-winning FA Cup Final goal in 1998*

"I get a shiver when I think about the Double every now and then, but my philosophy is simple. What is past is gone. What is important is what lies ahead."

1998 Double winning captain **Tony Adams**

"There are more skilful right-backs, better tacklers, more accurate passers and certainly those with a better first-time control of the ball. But when it comes to concentration, commitment and maximising what you've got, then Lee takes some beating."

George Graham *in his autobiography about Lee Dixon*

❝I am not worried about Premiership football, I came here fully aware that English football is very physical and full of tackling. It is a style of play that will suit me just fine.**❞**

Patrick Vieira *sends out a warning on the day he signs for Arsenal*

'Patrick Vieira is simply the king of midfield players in the English game. Not one player can get near him.**'**

Michael Thomas *likes Patrick Vieira too*

❝Robert Pires was quick
to emphasise that he is
not Marc Overmars, he is
Robert Pires and we must
not forget that.❞

Lee Dixon *knows that Robert Pires is Robert Pires*

‘When I first heard the fans chanting, I thought they were booing me. But I soon understood what they were saying and that they like me.’

Kanu(uuuuuuu)

"ARSENAL WIN THE WORLD CUP"

Daily Mirror *headline salutes Arsenal's (France's) 1998 World Cup win*

❛That's what they teach you at Arsenal. You have to win, wherever you play – home or away, youth team, reserves or first team – you have to win a football match.**❜**

Paul Merson

'Those that say it is the taking part and not the winning that is important are, for me, wrong. It is the other way round.'

Tony Adams

❝I used to enjoy movies and going to the theatre, but I don't have much time for that now. My way of relaxing is to watch a football match on television at home. I suppose for most men that might cause trouble at home, but at least I have the excuse that it's my job!**❞**

Arsène Wenger

❝I love the crowd and the atmosphere that you can only get by being around a bunch of Londoners at Arsenal.**❞**

Roger Daltrey, *of The WHO*

"You can be feeling tired towards the end of a game, but the Arsenal crowd picks you up when they start cheering and that carries you through to the end."

Ray Parlour *on Arsenal's 12th man*

‘Ray is without doubt the funniest player I've ever trained with. It's so important to have players such as Ray involved with the group, for his contribution on the field and spirit of it. I only wish I could understand more of what he says.’

Gilles Grimandi *on Ray Parlour*

"To me, he will always be the Romford Pélé. "

Ray Parlour finds an admirer in **Marc Overmars**

"I vividly remember a nil-nil with Leeds. It was one of my all-time favourite matches – only an Arsenal supporter could say that of a goalless draw."

Ray Davies *of The Kinks*

❝It is not so enjoyable to score goals if the team does not win.**❞**

Freddie Ljungberg

Arsenal

❝Ian Wright, Wright, Wright. So good, they named him thrice.❞

Jonathan Pearce

'It's a magnificent club and they really do look after the people that work for them, not just the players.'

Kenny Sansom

❝ I've made my decision
and I just hope people
respect it. I could have
earned more money
by going abroad, but I felt
this was the place
to be. **❞**

Sol Campbell *on signing for Arsenal, 2001*

‟I don't understand the reaction, it is only a game when all is said and done and Sol is such a lovely lad.„

Pat Jennings, *who made the same move across North London*

‘Before I came here, I would speak to the Manchester United players and they told me what it was like. Now I know what they were talking about. No one will roll over in games when you are with Arsenal, but I have adjusted now. I am ready.’

Sol Campbell

❝We have all had more fun than this. Have you ever known a colder night?**❞**

Martin Keown *after the defeat by Shakhtar Donetsk in Moscow, November 2000*

❛Kenny Dalglish came on at the same time as me and everyone expected him to win it for Liverpool. But here I was, a ginger-haired nobody, setting up the winning goal for Arsenal.❜

Perry Groves *on the 1987 League Cup Final win over Liverpool*

❛Look at that, look at that.❜

John Motson *loses it describing a Liam Brady effort during Arsenal's 5–0 win at The Lane in 1978*

❝I think they thought I
had gone past my best,
so I had to leave.**❞**

Pat Jennings *leaves Tottenham and
still has four cup finals in him*

❝A move like this only happens once in a lifetime.**❞**

Clive Allen *signs for Arsenal from QPR for £1million and leaves two months later, without playing a competitive game, to go to Crystal Palace*

❝I never thought of taking him off. It's nothing to worry about, it gives the face character.**❞**

George Graham *after Andy Linighan, complete with broken nose, headed in the history-making winner in 1993 FA Cup Final replay*

That will always be a memory for everyone else I suppose. The winner's medal and scoring the goal are my memories.

Steve Morrow *reflects on being dropped by Tony Adams and breaking his collar bone after the 1993 League Cup Final replay*

❛You can practise penalties, but you can't recreate the pressure. I've taken a penalty against Man United in the Charity Shield and as I put the ball down I suddenly realised the goal looks as big as a matchbox.❜

David Seaman

❝Once we went a goal in front I knew we had a chance because our strength is keeping clean sheets. We had a team of heroes tonight and none more so than Alan Smith.❞

George Graham, *after 1994 Cup Winners' Cup Final win over Parma*

‟The tension I feel during a game is appalling. You would think it gets better as you get older, but it doesn't.**”**

John Challis, *aka Boycie of* Only Fools and Horses *is no plonker.*

'It's one–nil to the Arsenal. That's the way we like it.**'**

Some things never change – **George Allison**
in the film The Arsenal Stadium Mystery

"I have not a single bad word to say for The Arsenal – it is a great club to play for"

Charlie Nicholas

❝I was very very lucky to play for Arsenal and win all those trophies, but when people turned up for my testimonial in appreciation for what I had done for the club, it was very humbling. Very emotional, but is every time I go back to Highbury, even as a spectator.**❞**

Paul Merson

"I never had a proper chance to say farewell to the Arsenal fans. This will be a great opportunity to do it properly."

Ian Wright *before Lee Dixon's testimonial*

It was very nice for me to play in Ian Wright's testimonial! The occasion surpassed all of my dreams. Every player likes to think he is appreciated and the fans tonight were simply magnificent.

Lee Dixon *after Wrighty had stolen the limelight in his game against Real Madrid, November 1999*

“I can't wait to put the boots back on and step out in the old red and white of my beloved Arsenal.”

Ian Wright's *passion is still clear as he prepares for a Masters Tournament at the age of 37*

'We've had a lot of good times, but you don't know how good they are until you have the bad ones.'

Tony Adams

"It sounds ridiculous, but I always put my watch into the right pocket of my trousers. If anybody wants to nick it, they'll know where to look now I suppose."

Superstitious **Steve Bould**

❝I told my son Josh that
Howard Wilkinson wanted
Daddy to play for England.
He told my daughter Olivia and
they had tears in their eyes as
they asked me, "Does that
mean you're not going to play
for Arsenal any more?"❞

Lee Dixon *following a surprise England return*

❝Arsenal come streaming forward now in surely what will be their last attack…A good ball by Dixon, finding Smith…For Thomas charging through the midfield…Thomas…It's up for grabs now…Thomas…Right at the end…An unbelievable climax to the league season, well into injury time…The Liverpool players are down, abject…Aldridge is down,

Barnes is down, Dalglish just stands there, Nicol's on his knees, McMahon's on his knees…Suddenly it was Michael Thomas bursting through, the bounce fell his way, he lipped it wide of Grobbelaar and we ave the most dramatic finish maybe n the history of the Football League. **"**

Commentary by **Brian Moore**, *26 May 1989, as Michael Thomas scores to clinch the Championship, at Anfield*

❝ All that was on my
mind was Bruce
Grobelaar. I didn't think
about what rested on that
one shot. **❞**

Michael Thomas, *1989*

❛The football Arsenal play now is
what you dream of playing. It's
smooth and velvety.**❜**

Michael Thomas – *still a fan over ten years later.*

❛Kanu is feeling very down. He's very sad. It was an accident. We didn't want to cheat and Kanu didn't know what happened. He didn't understand at all because he's a very fair player.**❜**

Arsène Wenger *on the goal that never was against Sheffield United in the 1999 FA Cup*

❛It was a big mistake. They threw the ball for me and I was all on my own. I passed it and after that I don't know. I only realised something was wrong when the United players went up to the referee. I was not happy, they [Sheffield United] were not happy.❜

Kanu

❝It is obviously an unprecedented situation but one we could not ignore. Everybody in football will welcome Wenger's sporting gesture and he should be congratulated for it.**❞**

*FA spokesman **Steve Double** congratulates Arsenal on their offer to replay the game*

❝Kanu is Kanu. He is the man. He has the ability to do special things and I love to watch him play.❞

Thierry Henry

Arsenal

❝I always like to score near the 'keeper. I like to do my tricks and when I see the 'keeper, I have to take him on.**❞**

Kanu

❝I remember almost hitting the clock at Highbury and was ready to tell the manager that I wanted to go back on the wing, but I knew he believed in me and that was enough.**❞**

Thierry Henry *was not always confident in front of goal*

❝Nicholas Anelka did a lot for this club, especially in the year we won the Double. Up front, he and Dennis Bergkamp were fantastic. He also had the big responsibility of taking over from Ian Wright. People who don't know him have the wrong image of him. He is a lovely guy off the pitch and a tremendous player on it.❞

Patrick Vieira

'I would never play in England in another shirt other than Arsenal's.**'**

Patrick Vieira

❝When you see them keeping the manager, wanting to build a 60,000-seat ground, wanting to win things – that's the ambition I have...I believe in the chairman and the board. I believe they will put everything right to make Arsenal one of Europe's biggest clubs.❞

Patrick Vieira

‟It was a surprise, but a very pleasant one. I had not planned to become a football club manager.„

Arsenal physio **Bertie Mee** *is appointed Arsenal manager*

❛A wise, shrewd, hard little man...full of character and pride. No one's fool, a man-manager of top class.**❜**

Chairman **Denis Hill-Wood** *praises Bertie Mee*

‘Only the players are important. I am not important.’

A modest **Bertie Mee** *at the time of the 1971 Double*

❝Everyone knows I'm an Arsenal supporter, I watch them all the time, and for someone like myself who grew up standing on the terraces and then jumped over and played with the players I actually idolised was just fantastic.❞

Charlie George *on fulfilling his boyhood dreams*

"To play for the club you support is a dream come true."

Ashley Cole, *some 30 years later, shows the dreams remain the same*

❝I supported Chelsea,
but my Dad was a big
Arsenal fan so I went to
Arsenal and I owe my
Dad a lot for that.**❞**

Paul Merson *proves that sometimes you need a
little pointer in the right direction*

❝I did not have a choice, but I am so glad I was born an Arsenal supporter.**❞**

Stuart Barnes, *former England rugby international*

❛If you lose hope, or lose belief, you may as well get out of football.❜

George Graham

'It was of course very special for me to be made skipper. Captaining this fantastic club is a great honour, no matter what the occasion.**'**

Ray Parlour *on captaining the team in 2001*

❝Part of the English game is that it's physical and enjoyable and...everybody I invite from a foreign country who watches the game says exactly the same: "There's something special here..."❞

Arsène Wenger

❛Marriage usually
stabilises. It gives players
a natural discipline – they
have to go home.❜

Arsène Wenger

❝I've not had to tell people like Robert Pires, Thierry Henry and Sylvain Wiltord about the FA Cup because they saw with their own eyes how much it meant when we played Tottenham in the semi-final at Old Trafford.**❞**

Patrick Vieira

❝It was only 2–1, but the score does not reflect the total dominance we had over them. Even Spurs fans were saying afterwards that they couldn't believe it was only 2–1.❞

Bob Wilson *reflects on the 2001 FA Cup semi-final win*

❝The international game
does nothing for me – it is
the Gunners that turn
me on. **❞**

TV presenter **Lisa Rogers** *shows her true colours*

' Second in the league might be good enough somewhere else, but not at Arsenal. **'**

Martin Keown

Arsenal

'We nearly didn't sign
him because the letters
did not fit on his shirt.'

David Dein *on the signing of Giovanni
van Bronckhorst*

❝I want to explode with Arsenal. There are trophies to win and unless there is a change of heart from the club, I want to win some.**❞**

Sylvain Wiltord

❝To be frank, when I first arrived I didn't think I would end my career here, but I am very happy. I am playing better than I have ever played and I have to thank English football for that.❞

Robert Pires

❝When I came to England I knew I had the ability, but mentally I wasn't strong enough. You see someone like Tony Adams before a game...He prepares for a match like a warrior.**❞**

Thierry Henry

❝I enjoy my life in London. I love wearing the Arsenal shirt and I get very special feeling every time I put on. It is something in my heart and hope it is something that will stay with me. The matter is not only in m hands because if I stop scoring goals maybe the club will not wan me, but if I can still play, I would lik to spend all my career here.**❞**

Thierry Henry

*We all want to be the
best and I believe I can
be the best with Arsenal.
I have a long-term vision
for the club.*

Arsène Wenger

❝ I thought football's greatest honour was to captain England. I was wrong. It was to captain Arsenal today. **❞**

Joe Mercer *addresses a banquet after Arsenal were defeated in the FA Cup Final by Newcastle in 1952*

'Happy those who can remain at Highbury.'

From Emma *by* **Jane Austen**.
How could she have known?

Sources P5: *Herbert Chapman: Football Emperor*, Stephen Studd, Pe
Owen, 1981; p6: *Soccer Tactics*, Bernard Joy, 1956; p7: pre
conference October 1996; p8: *Official Arsenal Magazine*: Vol I, Issue
p9: *Official Arsenal Magazine*: Vol II, Issue 2; p10: *The Official Centen*
of Arsenal Football Club, Phil Soar & Martin Tyler, Hamlyn 1986; p
Arsenal Story, Tom Whittaker and Roy Peskett (Editor), Sport
Hardbacks, 1957; p12: ibid.; p13: *Alex James, Life of a Football Lege*
James Harding, Robson, 1992; p14: *That's the Way the Ball Bounc*
Frank McLintock with Terry McNeill, Pelham Bks 1969; p15: *D*
Telegraph, 23 October 2001; p16: *The Official Centenary of Arse*
Football Club; p17: ibid.; p18: *That's the Way the Ball Bounces*; p19: *7*
Official Centenary of Arsenal Football Club; p20: *Official Arse*
Magazine: Vol I, Issue 3; p21: *Official Arsenal Magazine*: Vol I, Issue
p22: *Official Arsenal Magazine*: Vol I, Issue 7; p23: *The Official Centen*
of Arsenal Football Club; p24: *Arsenal1970-71 The Story of the Dout*
1971; p25: *Official Arsenal Magazine*: Vol I, Issue 1; p26: *The Goo*
Issue 74, December 1996; p27: *Jack Kelsey Fan Cl*
www.arsenalarsenal.co.uk; p28: *David O'Leary*, David O'Leary and Mil
Mainstream, 1988; p29: *Herbert Chapman: Football Emperor*; p30: *7*
Times, 10 April 1999; p31: *Proud to Say That Name*, Amy Lawren
Mainstream, 1997; p32: *Official Arsenal Magazine*: Vol III, Issue 1; p
www.irnsports.net; p34: *Official Arsenal Magazine*: Vol II, Issue 5; p
Official Arsenal Magazine: Vol II, Issue 8; p36: *A Love Supreme*: Issue *
p37: ibid.; p38: www.independent.co.uk; p39: www.bbc.co.uk; p
Daily Mail, 9 May 2002; p42: Leeds United match programme, 8 A
1998; p43: *Hampstead and Highbury Express*, 10 December 2001; p
Charlie, Charlie Nicholas & Ken Gallacher, Stanley Paul, 1986; p45: *7*
Official Centenary of Arsenal Football Club; p46: *Official Arse*
Magazine: Vol II, Issue 5; p47: *Revelations of a Football Manager*, Te
Neill, Sidgwick & Jackson, 1985; p48: BBC Radio commentary, 19
p49: *Official Arsenal Magazine*: Vol II, Issue 2; p50: *Official Arse*

agazine: Vol II, Issue 3; p51: www.sport4ever.net; p52: press nference, 30 March 2002; p53: www.arsenal.com; p55: *Herbert apman: Football Emperor*; p56: Jack Kelsey Fan Club, w.arsenalarsenal.co.uk; p57: *Cliff Bastin Remembers*, Cliff Bastin & an Glanville, 1950; p58: Jack Kelsey Fan Club, w.arsenalarsenal.co.uk; p59: ibid.; p60: *Official Arsenal Magazine*: Vol ssue 1; p61: *Official Arsenal Magazine*: Vol II, Issue 11; p62: press nference 13 September 1997; p63: *Daily Mail*, 22 November 2000; 7: press conference 11 May 1991; p68: *Daily Express*, 30 September 96; p69: press conference 6 December 2001; p70: w.geocities.com; p71: *Evening Standard*, 18 October 1996; p72: ghbury & Islington Express*, 15 September 2001; p73: press nference 6 December 2001; p74: press conference 6 May 19991; p75: *ficial Arsenal Magazine*: Vol V, Issue 1; p76: *Official Arsenal Magazine*: l III, Issue 10; p77: *The Sun* 12 July 1997; p78: Emmanuel Petit's icial website; p79: www.icons.com; p80: press conference, 16 May 98; p81: www.angelfire.com/vt/overspeed; p82: *Sunday Times* (South ica), 12 June 1998; p83: *The Glory and the Grief*, George Graham, dre Deutsch, 1996; p84: press conference 14 August 1996; p85: senal v Liverpool programme 14 January 2002; p86: *Official Arsenal agazine*: Vol IV, Issue 3; p87: *Official Arsenal Magazine*: Vol IV, Issue 4; 8: *Daily Mirror*, 13 July 2000; p89: *Official Arsenal Magazine*: Vol II sue 2; p90: *The Guardian*, 6 April 2002; p91: press conference 25 May 01; p92: *Official Arsenal Magazine*: Vol IV, Issue 8; p93: *Official Arsenal agazine*: Vol I, Issue 4; p94: www.icons.com; p95: ibid.; p96: *Official senal Magazine*: Vol II, Issue 2; p97: www.arsenal.com; p98: Capital old Sport commentary; p99: Arsenal V Blackburn programme 22 ctober 2001; p100: *Official Arsenal Magazine*: Vol V, Issue 3; p101: senal v Juventus programme 4 December 2001; p102: *Official Arsenal agazine*: Vol V, Issue 3; p103: press conference 7 November 2000; 04: Arsenal v. Schalke, match programme 19 September 2001; p105:

BBC Commentary, 1978; p106: *Official Arsenal Magazine*: Vol III, Issue p107: press conference June 1980; p108: press conference 20 M 1993; p109: www.sportsillustrated.cnn.com; p110: *Official Arse Magazine*: Vol V, Issue 7; p111: press conference 4 May 1994; p1 *Official Arsenal Magazine*: Vol I, Issue 4; p113: *The Arsenal Stadi Mystery*, Thorold Dickinson, 1939; p114: *Official Arsenal Magazine*: Vo Issue 6; p115: press conference 8 November 1999; p116: pre conference 3 November 1999; p117: *The Times*, 3 November 19: p118: www.arsenal.com; p119: *Addicted*, Tony Adams, HarperColl Willow, 1999; p120: *A Love Supreme*: Issue 82; p121: *Official Arse Magazine*: Vol V, Issue 3; p122: ITV commentary, May 1989; p124: *Ne of the World* 27 May 1989; p125: Arsenal v Liverpool programme January 2002; p126: press conference 13 February 1999; p127: pre conference 13 February 1999; p128: FA press release, February 199 p129: www.btinternet.com; p130: ibid.; p131: press conference, November 2001; p132: *Daily Mail*, 11 January 2002; p1: www.arsenal.com; p134: *L'Equipe*, 24 January 2001; p135: *The Offic Centenary of Arsenal Football Club*; p136: ibid.; p137: *Daily Mail*, October 2001; p138: Arsenal v Liverpool programme 27 January 200 p139: *Official Arsenal Magazine*: Vol IV, Issue 8; p140: Arsenal v Ast Villa programme 9 December 2001; p141: *Official Arsenal Magazine*: V I, Issue 3; p142: *The Official Centenary of Arsenal Football Club*; p14 *Islington Gazette*, 1 November 2001; p144: www.leaguemanagers.co p145: press conference 15 May 2001; p146: press conference 4 Janu 2002; p147: Arsenal v Middlesbrough programme 29 December 200 p148: *Official Arsenal Magazine*: Vol IV, Issue 3; p149: www.arsen world.net; p150: press conference 20 June 2001; p15 www.satchmo.win-uk.net; p152: www.soccerage.com; p15 www.angelfire.com; p154: www.arsenal-world.net; p155: pre conference April 2002; p156: www.arseweb.com; p157: *Emma*, Ja Austen.